ANALYSIS

THE PSYCHOLOGY OF POWER.
> The urgency of the problem of energy and fatigue.
> The view of the physicist, and of the religious.
> The psychological view.

EVIDENCE OF EXTRAORDINARY POWERS.
> Illustrated from various fields.
> Conclusions from these illustrations:
>> (1) Existence of an ample re-supply of strength.
>> (2) Not attained by power of will.
>> (3) Originate in the instinctive emotions.

THE MENTAL FACTOR IN FATIGUE.

I. Mental origin of fatigue demonstrated by –
  (a) Experiments in hypnotic suggestion.
  (b) Experiments in physiology.
  These prove the importance and priority of mental fatigue.
  Biological reasons why mind is fatigued before the body

II. Forms of fatigue:
  (1) Physical fatigue.
  (2) Over-sensitiveness of mind to physical fatigue. Application of this to everyday life.
  (3) False interpretation of mental fatigue as physical.
  (4) Purely mental fatigue, due to mental conflict.

THE INFIRMITY OF THE WILL.
> Power does not originate in the will.
> Illustrations to prove impotence of will against conviction and suggestion.
> Evil habits unconquered.
> Will requires power of the emotions.

THE INSTINCTS.
> The force of ideas; will; emotions.
> Instinctive emotions the real driving force of our lives.
> The importance of instincts in modern life.
>
> Policy of suppression a false one. Passion necessary in morality and religion.

THE INSTINCTS AND MORALITY.
> Is power derived from the instincts moral?
>> (1) Many instincts in themselves beneficent, e.g. maternal
>> (2) Instincts apparently anti-social may be directed to useful ends.
>> (3) In the long run the maximum power is gained when instincts are harmonized and directed by the reason toward worthy ends.

THE CONFLICT OF INSTINCTS.
> Of will and emotion: of emotion with emotion.
> Illustration.
> Minor conflicts exemplified in worry and anxiety.

THE CONVERSION OF THE INSTINCTS.
> Living beings raise the potential of energy.
> Illustration of the conversion of the instincts and instinctive emotions.
> Hunting:curiosity; pugnacity
> Fear: necessary fear; morbid fear; fear that stimulates.
> Sex: its overflow into the parental instinct.
> Self-assertion: aggression; submission; confidence.

CONFIDENCE AND FAITH.
> Derived from instincts of self-assertion.
> Essential to success and power.
> Illustrations.

THE EXPENDITURE OF POWER.
> Damming up the flow of energy leads to stagnation and fatigue.
> The inspiration of a purpose.
> Strength comes to those who expend it.

ENERGY AND REST.
> The cause of fatigue in mental conflict.
> The remedy is mental quietude.
> The characteristic neurasthenic.
> Physiological law of alternation of activity and rest.
>
> The art of resting.

THE SOURCE OF ENERGY.
> Physiological, psychological, and philosophical theories.
> Summary.

THE DYNAMIC OF RELIGION.
> The power of the Christian religion in abolishing conflict and directing the instinctive energies to high purposes.
> Power characteristic of primitive Christianity.
> Restfulness and peace also characteristic.
> Christianity as a moral healing force.

CONCLUSION.

THE PSYCHOLOGY OF POWER

BY

Capt. James .A. HADFIELD, M.A., M.B.

ASHHURST NEUROLOGICAL WAR HOSPITAL, OXFORD

THE PSYCHOLOGY OF POWER

THE increasing pressure of modern life, with its anxieties and cares, constitutes an ever-augmenting tax upon our strength. It is hardly surprising that nervous breakdowns are common, and that neurasthenia, or nerve fatigue, is the most significant disease of the age. Yet while, on the one hand, we see men and women so ill-adapted to fact the demands of life that the slightest exertion produces fatigue; on the other, we are called upon to witness exhibitions of power which fill us with wonder. The increasing demand for the power and energy requisite to face the strain compels us to investigate the sources of their supply. The purpose of my study is to direct attention to the problem of the sources of human energy and power.

It is commonly supposed that in each of us there is a reservoir, as it were, containing a certain supply of energy. This energy is said to be derived from the food we eat and the air we breathe, and to be, therefore, strictly limited in amount. When our expenditure is excessive our supply of energy runs very low, and we consequently suffer from a feeling of fatigue. Such is the theory of the physicist. The natural consequence of this belief in the physical character and the limited supply of our energy is that we are careful to economise our little store of strength, to husband our resources, lest by excess of expenditure we find the springs of our life run dry.

In contrast with this view, there have been men, and chiefly among them religious men, who have held that if our powers seem to fail, it is not because all the energy available is used up, but because its flow is checked, either by the channel being blocked up or by our inability to use it aright. *The chief cause of fatigue is not exhaustion but stagnation.* The way to power, therefore, is not to harbour our resources and store up our strength by inactivity, but to find the way to tap the resources of power at our disposal, so that they may flood our life and fill us with energy.

Of the two theories above stated modern psychology tends, on the whole, to support the second. At least the fact that (whatever their ultimate origin) there are resources of power, whose existence we do not ordinarily recognise but which can be made available for the purposes of our daily life, is one which has been firmly established by the scientific researches of recent years. In this Essay I propose, in the first place, to produce evidence of the existence of resources of power normally untapped; secondly, I shall show that these are psychic rather than physical in character; and, after discussing their relation to the instinctive emotions and to the will, shall consider the means by which they can be made available.

Evidence of Extraordinary Powers

I cannot do better than introduce the subject to the reader by one or two illustrations. A patient of mine, a tailor by trade, was buried by a high explosive shell in France. One of the striking features of his case was extreme weakness, the slightest exertion or a short walk producing fatigue. In the course of the treatment I induced him under hypnosis to remember the details of the incident, and made him live through it all again – the terrifying explosion, the debris burying him up to his neck, and a great baulk of timber tottering above his head in act to fall. By the recollection of these things he was thrown into a condition of extreme terror, and began to fight like a madman, flinging himself on the floor and dragging the bed down over him, seizing a heavy armchair and flinging it across the room, and generally putting forth such extraordinary strength that it required four men to hold him down. The strength he exhibited appeared almost superhuman, and it was quite beyond his voluntary power, for when he was awake his greatest exertion of will served only to emphasise his weakness and impotence. Furthermore, when he was wakened from the attack, far from being fatigued, he was relieved and refreshed, and spontaneously told me how much better he felt.

Similar exhibitions of strength are quite common in men swayed and mastered by a great emotion. Such strength is typical also of madness, in which strong bonds are broken, iron bars are wrenched loose, and extraordinary feats of endurance are performed. What is the secret of such power? In all these cases men seem to be tapping resources of strength, whether from within or from without, which, if we could discover and use, would rescue us from feeble ineffectiveness to a life of untold possibilities. We look upon such an exhibition of strength with much the same feelings as when we behold the lightning rend the heavens and tear up oaks by the roots – if only we could seize and store up such energy and devote it to the uses of our daily life.

The endurance and strength of men fighting against fearful odds when they are "up against it" is notorious, and many instances could be given from the war. Another of my patients had suddenly found himself in a trench containing six Germans. Realising that he was cornered he fought with fury, and succeeded in killing three of them before he was stunned by one of the survivors. A corporal, whose courage won the V. C., was for several days cut off from our troops, was exposed the whole time to bombardment (subsisting meanwhile on the barest rations), and yet, in spite of the awful strain, he came out feeling cheerful, elated and without fatigue. Several men with him had the endurance to pass through the same experience, but at the end were exhausted and broke down. The corporal had evidently discovered sources of power which were not exhausted by the terrible strain he underwent, but provided an ample re-supply.

One of my patients, suffering from an obstinate neurasthenia, asked for leave one day because his wife, the mother of six little children, had fallen ill with pneumonia consequent on influenza, and, owing to the epidemic, could secure no doctor except for the one visit in which her condition had been diagnosed. He had been a most despondent and depressed individual, scarcely ever speaking to any one else in the ward, still suffering from the tiredness and exhaustion typical of neurasthenia. He returned some days after, looking bright and cheerful, and almost his first words to me were, "I shall never doubt the power of prayer again, sir." In addition to the worry with the children, he had had the great anxiety of nursing his wife through a very serious illness without the aid of a doctor, and had been up day and night in his devoted labours. It is only those who have passed through a strain of that kind who now what it means; but it is equally true that they alone know the mighty resources that come to our aid in the time of extremity. In this case, his keenness to bring about the recovery of his wife, and the conviction of divine assistance, buoyed him up during the time of anxiety; and after the strain was over, the exhilaration of triumph saved him from the relapse that people too often bring on themselves by their lack of confidence.

Four years ago, at midnight, I witnessed an explosion at a great munition factory, and afterwards heard that a woman, after her day's work had risen from bed and, in anxiety for the safety of her husband and son, had run practically the whole distance of seven miles to the scene of the explosion in an incredibly short time.

William McDougall quotes the case of a boy who, being chased by a furious animal, leaped a fence which he could never afterwards scale even as a grown man, and after continuous athletic training. The emotion of fear liberated powers which his strength of will could never equal.

The reader will be able to add many, and perhaps more striking, cases than those I have mentioned. Most men, indeed, have experienced the invigorating effect of an overmastering emotion whose power is expressed not only in mental vigor, but in *physical* manifestations – the hot rush of blood in the veins, the quickening pulse, the deep strong breathing, the quivering nerve, the tense muscle, and the inrush of power which fortifies the soul and renders it quick to act an brave to endure.

Glancing over these illustrations of extraordinary powers, we are struck with three outstanding facts.

(1) Under certain conditions *extraordinary expenditure of energy can take place without equivalent fatigue.* It is generally assumed that such outbursts of power must end in a relapse leaving the exhausted man or woman broken in health. This undoubtedly often occurs, but is by no means necessary, and did not in fact occur in the cases that I have quoted from my own experience. The fatigue consequent on great exertion seems to bear no necessary relation to the amount of energy expended. One can become fatigued, like the neurasthenic, on very slight exertion; but, on the other hand, as in these cases, men, essentially no different from ourselves, are seen to exhibit extraordinary powers without any apparent fatigue. The successful issue of a great endeavour causes the gladness of victory to refresh the soul. This fact suggests to us the hypothesis that, while our energy is being used up, there is an ample store of energy to take its place if we could but discover and conform to the law of its supply: "the barrel of meal wastes not, neither does the cruse of oil fail." The power which can sustain us during the trial can renew our strength when victory is won.

(2) We observe that *these powers are greater than any at the disposal of the conscious will*. The most strenuous efforts to walk made by the soldier who had been buried ended only in weakness; the athlete could never leap the fence again; the patient who has passed through the time of anxiety and strain with his wife's illness felt that, though his will was feeble, some other power laid hold of his life and gave it strength.

(3) As to *the origin of these powers* those who experience them can give no more account than the onlooker. In olden times such outbursts of strength were looked upon sometimes as being due to possession by evil spirits: at other times, as in the story of Samson, the amazed beholders exclaimed, "The spirit of the Lord came mightily upon him." To the scientific observer, however, there is one very significant phenomenon. On every case these powers are associated with one of the *fundamental instinctive emotions* – whether of fear in the buried soldier and the athlete, tenderness in the husband and the wife, or in the other cases, the instincts of self-preservation and pugnacity. It would look as if it were only when instinctive emotions like these are arouse that energies are liberated adequate to sweep away all obstacles and take complete mastery of our lives.

These points we shall discuss in order, taking up first the question of fatigue, then illustrating the infirmity of the will, and, lastly, the power of the instinctive emotions.

THE MENTAL FACTOR IN FATIGUE

If we are to discover the sources of strength we must first investigate the causes of fatigue. There is a fatigue that comes from the body, and a fatigue that is of the mind; and these two forms of fatigue are very closely associated in experience, although they are separable in origin. Disappointment will leave us tired out. The desert traveller is about to fall exhausted, when the sight of an oasis will revive his spirits and give him energy to plod on for miles. A mile walk with a bore is more fatiguing than twenty miles with the lady of your choice.

We have already observed in the illustrations of extraordinary powers – the endurance of men fighting with their backs to the wall, or buoyed up by a great hope that great emotions can endow men and women with almost superhuman strength. On the other hand, the neurasthenic, tired with the slightest exertion, is suffering from a fatigue due sometimes to discouragement, sometimes to stagnation of the mind, rendering the body lifeless and inert, sometimes to discouragement resulting from a conviction of bodily debility. This is the type of fatigue from which most of us normally suffer. It may take the form of a feeling of boredom, of *ennui*, of the want of ideals and ambitions, which makes the soul limp and exhausts the body; or it may express itself in a helpless inability to cope with work in which we are really interested. In all these instances it can be shown that it is the mind that has flagged and become fatigued; when the mind is revived it finds the body ready and prepared to answer to its call.

The mental origin of fatigue may be illustrated by two experiments – the one psychological, the other physiological. (*a*) In the first, an experiment in hypnotic suggestion, we shall see how either fatigue or strength of body can be brought about purely by a mental attitude. (*b*) In the second, an experiment first devised by Mosso, we shall see that of all the functions that come into play in the performance of any action, the mind is the first to be fatigued; and it is therefore with fatigue of the mind that we have to concern ourselves most.

(*a*) Before describing the experiment in hypnotic suggestion it is, perhaps, well to say that the old view that in hypnosis some virtue, fluid, or power goes out from the hypnotiser to the subject, is now completely discredited. The essential feature of hypnotic suggestion is the communication of an idea to the mind of the patient; by hypnotic suggestion we inhibit for the moment the critical powers of the mind, and get the mind into such a condition of receptivity that any idea introduced into it is accepted without question and, for the time being, holds complete sway. The hypnotist does not, as is sometimes supposed, impose his will upon a reluctant subject; he merely suggests an idea to the mind of the patient under conditions which predispose the patient to accept and appropriate it as his own.

To illustrate this point I may be pardoned for quoting the words of a patient. "When I came," he writes "I thought I was going to be doped; that you were going to put something in me, perhaps something I did not like. Now I know that I have lived for years in a cellar; you have lifted me out and liberated what was in me."

To return to my experiment, I asked three men to submit themselves to test the effect of mental suggestion on their strength, which was measured by gripping a dynamometer. I tested them (1) in their normal waking condition; (2) after suggesting to them under hypnosis that they were "weak"; (3) after suggesting under hypnosis that they were "very strong". In each case the men were told to grip the dynamometer as tightly as they could – that is to say, to exert the will to the utmost. Under hypnosis the mind is very suggestible, and the response to the suggestions of weakness and strength gave very remarkable results. In the normal waking condition the men gave an average grip of 101 lbs. When, under hypnosis, I had given the men the idea that they were very weak, the average grip was only 29 lbs., one of them, a firefighter, remarking that his arm felt "tiny, just like a baby's." My suggestions of strength produced an average grip of 142 lbs. as against the 101 lbs. which was the best they could do in their normal waking conditions. A second test, measured by the time occupied in holding out a weight, gave similar results. In brief, when I suggested "weakness," the full flood of energy was checked and the men were capable of only one-third of their normal strength, whereas by suggestion of "strength" latent powers were liberated and their normal strength increased by half as much again.

Such an experiment shows us that, when our minds are depressed with the idea of weakness, our strength may be diminished by two-thirds; whereas if we have the stimulus of a great inspiration our strength may thereby be increased by one half. It is a conclusion of the utmost importance for practical life. The weakness that overtook the men when they felt they were weak is exactly what we observe in those suffering from neurasthenia. In these men there was produced an artificial neurasthenia. The neurasthenic, whose tiredness makes him a burden to himself and to every one else, is in the same case as these three men when their minds were obsessed by the idea of weakness so that they could grip only 29 lbs. He, like them, is physically strong, but he is overmastered by the feeling the he has no strength, and therefore is easily fatigued. The radical defect, both in the neurasthenic and in these three men when weakness was suggested, is in the mind. They *believed* they were weak and fatigued, and this belief produced the reality. According to their faith was it done to them. Once let the mind lose confidence in its strength, and its energy flows away like water.

On the other hand, the condition of the three men when, being obsessed with the idea of strength, they could grip 142 lbs. illustrates the cases of men of whom we have given examples, who were possessed of an abnormal energy for which they themselves could not account, but which made them capable of almost incredible feats of strength and endurance.

It would seem, then, that the limits of strength in our daily lives are defined less by the body than by the mind, and that the resources of power are psychic rather than physical in character.

(*b*) Mosso's famous experiment proves that, of all the factors involved in the performance of any action, the mind is the first to be fatigued. In an ordinary voluntary action, say, the moving of an arm, the impulse passes from the mind and will by means of the cells of the brain, down the nerves, passing through the nerve-endings to the muscle. By stimulating the nerve with electric shocks, one can produce contractions of the muscle, but after a time these contractions cease, owing to fatigue; but if the muscle alone is then stimulated, the muscle continues to contract. That is to say, it is not the muscle that has been fatigued. By similar experiments it is proved that neither is it the nerve nor the nerve-cell that first is fatigued, but the nerve-ending; indeed, the nerve-cell and the nerve are found to be almost unfatiguable. But press the experiment a stage further and the more important question then arises, whether the fatigue may not be psychic rather than physical in origin. *Is it the mind or the nervous system that is first fatigued?* Mosso's experiment helps to decide this question. A man's fatiguability is tested by tying a weight to his finger and making him flex and extend the finger until the onset of fatigue prevents him moving his finger any more. If the nerve to the finger is then immediately stimulated by a weak electric current, without giving time for the fatigue to pass off, the finger continues to flex and extend. In other words, the fatigue does not originate in nerve, nerve-ending, or muscle, which are all still quite active, but in the will.[1] The mind is fatigued, whereas the body is prepared to go on: the flesh is willing, but the spirit is weak.

The deduction that we draw from this experiment is that *the mind is exhausted before the body*. And this fact, strange as it may seem at first sight, is explicable on biological grounds, and that for two reasons.

The first reason is obvious. The mind is the latest part of the human organism to have developed in evolution, and is therefore the least completely adapted to its environment. In the face of the chances and rebuffs of life it frequently finds itself nonplussed; it cannot live as it would because of the limitations surrounding it; it turns away sick at the problems it has to face. From time to time we actually get cases from the seat of war of men who have "regressed" to childhood, behaving almost exactly as children of two or three years old. In these cases the mind, unable any longer to endure the strain of living under such conditions, becomes tired out and reverts once again to the golden age of a protected infancy.

The second biological reason would appear to be that the body may be protected from exhaustion. The susceptibility of them to fatigue is valuable in warning the body of its approach to the danger zone, and so preventing the body from going too far. If it were not for this warning we might sometimes be carried away by our enthusiasm. The man of genius has, indeed, an extraordinary capacity for work, because his mind is inspired by a great enthusiasm; but his inspiration might urge him to deeds too strenuous for his outworn body, and the world would perhaps be poorer for his loss. Thus nature determines that the mind shall normally be fatigued first, so that he will not put too great a strain on the body. But in the majority of men (if we may assume that the majority are not men of genius) such mental fatigue occurs long before we get anywhere near the danger zone of bodily fatigue, and the body is rarely given the opportunity of showing the extent of its endurance.

[It is possible, of course, to hold that toxins formed in the body poison the brain (see below, on Physical Fatigue) and thus produce the fatigue, but it is inconceivable that the amount of waste products from the exercise of one finger could have such wide-reaching effects.]

The discussion so far has put us in the position of being able to affirm the dominant influence of the mind in the production of fatigue, and to sum up *the four main forms of fatigue*: (1) Purely physical fatigue; (2) Over-sensitiveness of the mind to physical fatigue; (3) False interpretation of mental fatigue as physical; (4) Purely mental fatigue, chiefly due to the conflict in the mind itself between will and emotion, or between the different emotions themselves.

(1) *Physical fatigue* – Fatigue and neurasthenia are very frequently caused by poisons such as those from tuberculosis, cancer, or intestinal sepsis. Further, during the exercise of the muscles there are formed certain waste products which are supposed gradually to poison the nervous system; and after a great physical effort changes are seen to take place in the nerve-cells. There are, again, cases in which the mind's activity outstrips the body in strength. This has been observed in birds flying across the continent, in whom the instinct of migration is so strong that it outdoes the body and the birds fall dead with exhaustion. This also occurs occasionally in men whom some great enthusiasm or passion for reform drives on to reckless neglect of their strength, till they are compelled to rest their bodies in eternal sleep. But the psychological experiment in hypnotic suggestion, as well as the physiological experiments quoted above, show that at any rate the greater part of the fatigue from which we suffer is of mental origin; in fact, exhaustion of purely physical origin is rare.

(2) *The over sensitiveness of the mind to physical fatigue* – In the course of our daily life we more often feel fatigued because we are too sensitive to this physical tiredness; we take notice of its symptoms when we ought to neglect them. Normally there are thousands of impressions and sensations in our body which ought never to reach consciousness but should be dealt with by the lower brain centres, such as the beating of the heart, the movements of the stomach, the sense of position of our limbs, and the sensation of normal fatigue in our body. But sometimes, owing to some exceptional experience – palpitation through fear, indigestion, or extreme physical exhaustion – these sensations force their way into consciousness, and having once gained a footing, continue to claim the conscious attention of the mind. The mind begins to pay undue heed to these sensations, and pseudo-angina pectoris, nervous dyspepsia, and neurasthenia with its oversensitiveness to fatigue result. Even with reasonably healthy people them ind may at certain times be responsible for the fatigue felt in that it may be oversensitive to the tiredness of the body and, by forcing it into consciousness, may exaggerate what should be a trifling and transient sensation into a feeling of complete exhaustion. Normal fatigue of body, like all the other thousand routine sensations of the body, should never reach consciousness except under very exceptional circumstances. The healthy individual comes in from a long, pleasant

walk, and, though his body may be tired, he takes no notice of it and is quite happy. The neurasthenic, perhaps owing to some exceptional experience of over-fatigue in the past, but more often through introspection, becomes over-sensitive to these sensations. The same amount of waste products are probably formed in each of the men after the same length of walk, but, while the healthy man neglects, the neurasthenic notices his tiredness, and therefore suffers from exhaustion. Under hypnotic suggestion a pin-prick can be made to feel like the stab of a dagger, and the lifting of a book can cause complete exhaustion, because the mind is rendered over-sensitive by suggestion. Similarly the man who is always expecting fatigue will find what he looks for. The slightest thing tires him, but only because he is sensitive to the slightest thing. He turns the molehill into a mountain, and this mountain goes into labour and brings forth neurasthenia.

(3) Meanwhile we need to point out that *fatigue of purely mental origin is often misinterpreted and is attributed to a physical origin*. Man has not yet learnt to discriminate clearly between mental and physical sensations. Hence mental pain tends to express itself in terms of physical injury. Thus when we receive bad news the shock is primarily mental, but our mind subconsciously finds a physical expression for the pain and localises it in the head, with the result that we get a nervous headache; but this is because our mind has no other way of finding for a "mental pain" a local habitation and a name. This is the explanation of not a few apparently physical, but really functional, diseases. For this reason, when the mind is itself fatigued by worry, anxiety, depression, or fear, this fatigue, though purely mental, is often *felt* to be physical, and we have the same sensations as if it were the body that was tired out.

(4) *Purely mental fatigue* is chiefly due to the conflict in the mind between the instincts and the will, or between the instincts themselves, and is of the greatest importance not only in the study of the causes of fatigue but for the acquisition of power. The powerful instincts crave for free expression; the will attempts to hold them down; the house is divided against itself and cannot stand. The instinctive emotions conflict with another, and the struggle for mastery robs our lives of strength and leaves us prostrate. This inner conflict, the chief cause of fatigue, and its cure, we shall study in a later section.

To call fatigue mental rather than physical is not to suggest that it is "unreal." Mental fatigue is the *most* real and the most important for our lives. It follows that those who would live lives of energy must look to the resources of the mind rather than those of the body, and must study the laws which condition mental energy and mental fatigue.

The Infirmity of the Will

It is generally considered that it is only by force of will that we exercise power; and in recent years the glorification of will power has been characteristic of certain philosophers, mainly of Teutonic origin, and has been exploited by advertisers in pictures of square-jawed, clenched-fisted supermen. But is the will in point of fact as potent as popular theory would have us believe? My own hospital ward, as well as those of every physician of the mind, is full of examples of will that fails to accomplish what it wills. We are constantly dealing with cases where a man tries his utmost to perform certain actions and fails to do them; and yet they are perfectly possible to him.

I had a patient, a healthy lad of twenty, who had been engulfed in the marshes of the Piave and was invalided home paralysed in both legs. When put on his feet he was absolutely terror-stricken, and was with the greatest difficulty supported by two men. He frequently attempted to walk, exerting his will and determination to the utmost, but his attempts all ended in failure and distress. As there was no actual disease of the nervous system I treated him under hypnosis by hypnotic suggestion, and a few weeks later he was playing football. The desire to walk was there; effort of will to walk was there; but these could not cure him – the will was impotent to save.

[This has been stated as follows by Couè "Where will and imagination conflict, it is always imagination that wins." This I believe is a fallacious statement and have criticised it in "Nature 1923."]

Another lad, whom I treated only a few days ago, suffered from a bullet wound through the shoulder, which, however, did not injure any important nerve, but paralysed his whole arm. I hypnotised him, and in less than two minutes had restored the power which had been lacking for months. His greatest effort to move it had resulted again in failure; yet movement proved to be possible. Again, where the will was impotent, some other power succeeded.

[It is only right that I should mention that "shell-shock" cases are more dramatic in their symptoms and in their cure than we can hope for in civilian patients, where the disease is often of long standing, its cause difficult to expose, and its cure proportionately more difficult.]

To revert back to my illustrations: the man who in fright leaped the fence, the patient who struggled so violently that four men were needed to keep him down, the man fighting with his back to the wall, were all able to do things which by the greatest effort of will they could never have accomplished. On the other hand, I have been in my ward speaking casually with the men when suddenly I have told one man that he could not rise from his chair but was stuck to it; another that he could not move his arm; another that he felt compelled to stand on one leg; and it was ludicrous to observe the strenuous efforts they made to act contrary to may suggestions. They exercised their wills, but to no effect. The performances of public hypnotists abound with such experiments; my only excuse for doing them is that I may convince men whom I want to heal of the power of suggestion, even in the absence of hypnosis.

Let me refer again to my hypnotic experiment in fatigue. As each man gripped the dynamometer I told him to do so "as hard as ever he could." Yet a man would one minute be able to do only 29 lbs., and a few minutes after he could manage 142 lbs. It is quite obvious that the difference in power was due, not to the exercise of the will, which was strained to the utmost in each case, but to some force that the will was impotent to affect. We shall observe, later, that this obstacle to the full exercise o the will *was the belief that the thing attempted was impossible*.[1] This breakdown of the will accounts for a large number of the nervous ills and morbid habits with which the physician has to deal. Sometimes it takes the form of perversion. I have a patient who, when trying to move his right leg, invariably moves his left leg. He observes his mistake but cannot correct it. There is a want of co-ordination somewhere; the couplings have gone wrong.

But I have only to appeal to the reader to look into his own life to realise how futile is the will to help us in many of our difficulties. Our attempts to prevent blushing produce only a deeper crimson; the effort to be at our ease produces a strained attitude; and in moral actions how often does our greatest determination to do right end in failure? It was long ago one discovered "what I would, that do I not; but what I hate, that I do." One thing is willed, another is performed. The victim of a moody or irritable temper, or of some evil habit, spends days and nights in vain endeavour to master it. What more pathetic sight than that of a confirmed drug-taker affirming with a sickly smile that he can easily give it up when he wants to. A vulture was seen to be feeding on a carcass as it floated down the Niagra river above the Falls; when the danger-point came it doubtless expected to spread its wings and fly off; but when, in fact, it spread its wings, it found that it could not rise; its talons were frozen to the carcass on which it fed, and so it was carried over the Falls to its doom. So the victim of evil habits tells you, "I am all right, you don't need to bother about me; I can give it up when I want to"; but when he rises to shake himself and put on strength, he finds his will power has gone. The freedom of the will may be a doctrine which holds true of the healthy, and, indeed, the exercise of will and determination is the normal way in which to summon the resources of power; but the doctrine that the will alone is the way to power is a most woe-begone theory for the relief of the morally sick – and who of us is whole? Freedom to choose? Yes! But what if, when we choose, we have no power to perform? We open the sluice-gates, but the channels are dry; we pull the lever, but nothing happens; we try by our will to summon up our strength, but no strength comes

> We cannot kindle when we would
> The fire that in the soul resides

Will and determination are, of course, essential to moral endeavour, and without them the instincts would run riot. When we say "I will," we feel an accession of power that enables us to conquer, and we attribute that power to the will. But the futility of looking to the will *alone* for our source of strength is obvious, and those who rely on it are running the risk of disaster; for particular action the will is dependent on some other power. As long as it acts in conformity with this power all is well. Under these circumstances the more strenuous the will, and the greater our resolution and determination, the greater will be our strength. But if it conflicts with this power, as in our illustrations, the will is impotent. The energies which give the driving force to our lives are not derived from the will, but from another source: they will be found to have their origin in the instinctive emotions. As we shall observe later, the function of the will is to direct and work in conformity with the potent forces, derived from the instinctive emotions, and to regulate the release of these forces waiting ready for action.

This view of the will suggests two conclusions of great importance for religion. (1) An evil deed is not always due to an "evil will" for which one is to be held responsible, but may be due to impulses over which the will has no control, or to distortions of character which the will is unable to set right, and it is only just that the offender should be treated as sick rather than sinful. (2) We cannot rely upon the will alone to deliver us from evil habits. Modern psychotherapy confirms the old religious belief that to give power to the will, confidence and faith in the possibility of victory are essential.

[I would suggest that the "cure of souls" is a practice too seriously neglected by the modern church.]

The Instincts

The great driving forces of life are the Instinctive Emotions. The Will may open the sluice-gates, but the Instinctive Emotions constitute the flood which sweeps through the channel. Great ideas may sway masses of men as when the cry of "Liberty, Equality, and Fraternity" called thousands to rise in revolution; yet it is only when associated with an emotion, and particularly an instinctive emotion, that the idea is charged with compelling power.

[On the subject of the instincts and their practical bearing on human life. I would urge the reader, if he has not yet done so, to study W. McDougall's *Social Psychology*, for it is so to Dr. McDougall that we owe the recognition of the paramount importance of the instincts in social life. That book shows how intimately connected are the instincts and certain great emotions, and I use the term Instinctive Emotion to indicate such emotions as Fear, Tenderness, Wonder, which are racially inherited and primitive, and therefore can dominate our whole human life and conduct.]

The instinctive emotions give driving force to the will and put life into great ideas, and, being liberated like the winds from the cave of Acolus, burst forth, either to do their work of destruction or, if rightly controlled, to speed us, with full-bellied sail, on the voyage to the harbour of our destiny.

When we look back on our previous illustrations of extraordinary powers we see that the *main* forces acting in and through these men were the instinctive emotions. Fear , the expression of the instinct of self-preservation, gave the soldier, buried in the debris and and fighting for his life, almost superhuman power. The instinct of pugnacity gave one desperate man surrounded by the enemy the strength of five. The instinctive emotion of fear enabled the athlete to make a spring which he could never afterwards accomplish by power of will alone. In these cases the driving force obviously comes from the instinctive emotions; and they are none the less at work in great reformers, statesmen, and industrial monarchs. Wilberforce could never have induced Britain to make so great a sacrifice in hard cash for the liberation of the slaves had he not appealed to an instinctive emotion which could sweep away thoughts of prudent economy. The emotion aroused in his own soul, and which he quickened in the soul of others, was the feeling of pity, an emotion characteristic of the parental instinct. ["Like as a father pitieth his own children."] The instinct of constructiveness combined with the instinct of self-assertion and the ambitious desire for power drives one man from the seculsion of a village to control the affairs of an empire, and another to organise a trust. It is when our feelings are aroused, when passion is awakened in the breast, when the approach of danger makes us alert to strike, when the sight of brutality to a child kindles our indignation, or when we are possessed by some soul-satisfying ambition, – it is then that we feel most deeply the sense of power. Not in the cold, deliberate choice of the will, but in the passion of he soul is to be found that flood of energy which can open us to the resources of power. Mastered by such a passion the soul will admit no defeat.

The strength of the instincts has not yet been fully appreciated, nor is it fully realised how great a part they play in common life. They have been boycotted by the cultured as brutish survivals, and even now some regard them as little more than a power that makes the birds migrate and the bees furnish the hive. Hardly do these people realise that society itself exists in response to an instinct of the herd, that their desire to travel is a response to the instinct of migration, and the impulse to build great cities and empires is the same impulse as compels the behavior to build the dam. The sociologist is most concerned with the gregarious instinct, so lucidly demonstrated by

Trotter in *The Instinct of the Herd*. Yet it is only recently that adequate recognition has been given by sociologists to the instincts. Fortunately we have now ceased to ignore them, and we realise that the instincts are the raw material upon the direction of which depends most of our individual and social life, and we now regard them for the most part as healthy. But even to this day many moralists adopt the prevailing attitude towards the instincts in advocating a stern suppression of them. Such an attempt is doomed to failure, for two reasons. Because, in the first place, it is practically impossible to suppress such deep rooted hereditary predispositions; and secondly, because the suppression of them would only dam up the channels of power which nature has provided. If we attempt to suppress our instincts, there is a conflict between will and impulse which ultimately destroys our harmony of soul.

Religious teaching has sometimes been guilty of this mistaken suppression. In their dread of emotionalism – the unruly debauch of unrestrained feeling – and its consequences in conduct, they have attempted to abolish all emotion as a thing either dangerous or vulgar. In doing so they have failed to appreciate that the Christian religion is founded on an emotion – the all-embracing emotion of love. To rob the soul of emotion is to deprive it of its driving force and leave it lifeless. Matthew Arnold's description of religion as being morality *tinged* with emotion is a delightful though unconscious satire on what religion actually is at the present day, but certainly not what it should be. A "tinge" of emotion is not the kind of thing to turn the world upside-down. "No heart is pure that is not passionate; no virtue is safe that is not enthusiastic." If religion means anything at all, it ought to mean the full and harmonious display and exercise of all our powers, emotional and intellectual, so that we present our whole selves a *living* sacrifice to God.

The Instincts and Morality

But if we accept the thesis that the instinctive emotions are, humanly speaking, the sources of our human energies, the question arises – Are these forces moral? Revenge and lust, as well as heroism, bring an enhancement of strength. If the instinctive emotions are the springs of power, can the sexual libertine lay claim to it as justifiably as the devoted mother? The blind rage of instinctive passion can scarcely be called moral, and yet it fills beast and man with extraordinary power.

The following observations are therefore necessary to a true estimate of the moral value of the instinctive emotions.

(1) In the first place, it must be recognised how many of the instincts have, in their very nature, a moral and altruistic tendency. The tenderness of a mother for her child, perhaps the most perfect example of an instinct in the whole of human life, is at the same time the most perfect example of a beneficent instinct. It is found not only in the human mother but in the lioness, the tigress, and the bird. Again, in the herd instinct, which makes the individual surrender all his personal claims to the demands of the pack, lie the germ and the source of most of the social virtues. The instincts are not brutal because they are shared by brutes, and, indeed, it might be urged that the noblest deeds of man have sprung from the altruistic instincts which originate in mother-love and loyalty to one's fellows and can be traced far back into the animal kingdom. But even such beneficent instincts need to be wisely directed. In the case of the maternal instinct, for instance, there comes the time when the child must no longer rely upon the mother but win independence. The lingering care of the mother for the grown-up daughter is certain at some time to clash with the impulse to independence in the daughter, and is the cause of what misunderstanding and consequent friction which so often brings unhappiness to both mother and daughter. They are both guided by instinctive impulses that are right and necessary – the one of maternal care, the other of independence. The friction which so often results would frequently be avoided were both mother and daughter to realise the causes of their misunderstandings. A wider knowledge of the influence of the instincts would materially assist in bringing about peace and harmony in everyday life. As soon as both mother and daughter *realise* that the opinions and desires of the other are not due to "sheer cussedness," but understand that such desires are instinctive and natural, so soon will this understanding bring about peace and forgiveness.

[The need for such understanding is most felt in regard to the instincts in growing children, whose impulses toward the expression of the instincts are so often treated as "naughtiness." The child naturally feels unjustly treated, for the impulse to obey the instincts, a perfectly beneficent impulse if wisely guided, is stronger than the impulse to obey the injunctions of the parent, whose business it ought to be to guide and not the repress the instincts and to make them amenable to the control of reason.]

(2) On the broadest definition, morality is that which is found to be valuable for social life. In the animal world all the instincts are, in this sense, moral. And, as we have seen, some of them, such as the tenderness of the mother for her young, or the loyalty of the individual to the pack, can, with but a little sublimation, become the basis of all that is best and highest in human life. Others, however, like the instinct of pugnacity, may seem in human society to have outlived their day. At an early stage of human evolution such an instinct was valuable in the struggle for existence. But this struggle, at least in its cruder form, is, or ought to be, a thing of the past; with the result that the instinct of pugnacity may easily lead to anti-social conduct. Nevertheless, every instinct, however ill-adapted to the requirements of present-day civilised life, has had value in its day in that it worked for the good of the species as a whole, and should be regarded, so far, as moral, or capable or being moralised. I shall deal with the question of the transformation and moralisation of the instincts in a later section.

(3) The moral potentialities of the force manifested in the instincts may be judged also from another point of view. The source of power lies not in instinctive emotion alone, but in instinctive emotion expressed in a way with which the whole man can, for the time being at least, identify himself. Ultimately, this is impossible without the achievement of a harmony of all the instincts and the approval of the reason an evil man has access to the same instinctive emotions as the good man, and may use them for wrong ends – as a Napoleon for his ambition, or a murderer for his hate. The man who gives vent to blind rage may feel the same satisfaction and relief as does the man who shows his indignation at some moral wrong. Yet in the long run those who misuse their powers destroy themselves by their very passions. It may be true that the man who takes personal vengeance on another may satisfy his instinct of revenge and feel elated, but he is apt to be so ostracised by his fellows that, quite independently of any practical inconvenience their consequent action toward him may entail, the herd instinct in him rises up in opposition to the instinct of revenge and sets

up an internal conflict which soon robs him of that harmony of the instincts which I shall show later on to be essential to power.[1] Thus the greatest and permanent power comes to him who uses it not for his own personal ends, but for the good of his fellows; for only by such a use of it does he achieve the maximum inner harmony. We may therefore assert that, while it is open to the evil man to give vent to a particular instinctive emotion, and thereby to lay claim for a moment to the power that nature lavishes upon those who use her gifts, it is only to those who use them alight that the greatest powers are given. Thus the powers at our disposal are not so neutral and non-moral as they seem, but tend to favour those who will use them for the noblest purposes. Revenge, pride, and passion destroy the permanent inner harmony of the soul, even though they may temporarily energise it into activity. Chivalry, honour, and love, devoted to the service of others, tend to produce a transformation of instincts and a living harmony of the soul which can permanently keep open the sluice-gates of power.

We shall proceed, then, to deal with the questions which have just arisen, and show how the crude forces which reside in the instinctive emotions can best be utilised for human endeavours and ideals. We shall first show how the instincts of the baser sort, if focussed on some dominating purpose or idea, may be transformed; after which we shall demonstrate the necessity of expending our powers as a pre-requisite of receiving more power, and finally we shall deal with the question of the conflict instincts, the abolition of which conflict is necessary to unity and to power.

THE CONFLICT OF INSTINCTS

The presence of conflict in the soul drains it of strength, and is one of the main causes of weakness. "I see another law in my members warring against the law of my mind." The conflict may be of instinctive emotions with ideas, as when a man is feeble because he is obsessed with intellectual doubt. At other times the weakness is due to the conflict of instinctive emotions and will, one of the most common forms of which is the attempt to suppress the instincts by the will, already referred to. But chiefly our powers are sapped because the instincts are divided against themselves. Let *one* instinct sway the mind and there is the sense of power. But the instincts are often opposed, and turn many of our best endeavours into failures. We are ambitious to succeed, but we are checked by the fear of making fools of ourselves. We never learn to skate, because we think of the ridiculous figure we should cut if we fell. Thus the desire to excel in any accomplishment (the instinct of self-assertion) conflicts with the possible feeling of shame and self-abasement.

The following case illustrates my point so well that I shall give it in some detail. I have recently been treating a lady who, when she came to me was so neurasthenic and easily fatigued that she habitually slept for sixteen hours out of the twenty-four. After a good night;s sleep from 9 P.M. till 7 A.M. she would rise and have breakfast, but the effort caused her so much fatigue that she would retire to bed again at 9 A.M. to sleep till 12. Now this was not laziness in the ordinary sense; she was an affectionate mother, and was anxious above all things to be able to work and play with her children, but she had not the strength. It was purely a case of mental fatigue, produced by a conflict of instinctive emotions.

Her cure could only be affected by discovering the cause and eradicating it from the mind. This process of discovery was conducted largely under hypnosis, since the patient could give little assistance in her waking state. It was discovered that the cause was the long-continued strain of nursing a very delicate child, when on more than one occasion it seemed that it must be a question of whether mother or child should be sacrificed. In her, then, two most powerful instinctive emotions had been at war, namely, the instinct of self-preservation and the maternal instinct. The result was a complete breakdown, several phobias, and a fatigue lasting some years, even though the original cause of anxiety was happily at an end. These were in turn removed, the instincts readjusted, the phobias explained; and the last account I have received from her husband, some months later, is to the effect that she is perfectly well.

[Other cases of conflict leading to nervous breakdown which have lately come under my notice may be briefly indicated. The sense of duty to her mother clashed with the instinctive desire for independence in a grown-up daughter, and a feeling of restless discontent resulted. Fear and the impulse to run away conflicted in the mind of the soldier with his sense of duty, and ended in a condition of paralysis of the legs, unconsciously produced, which solved the immediate problem but brought about a breakdown in health. The eagerness to please a master, with whom a patient of mine was in love, together with the constant sense of failure in this attempt, brought about a conflict between sexual instinct and self-pride, and produced a neurasthenia of many years' standing. A man's desire to live a clean and pure life was hampered by the shame of a past sin.]

Fortunately most of us are not called on to suffer from such conflicts, but conflict is nevertheless represented in everyday life by anxiety and worry. Anxiety is essentially a conflict of emotions. Anxiety about the future, about one's children, about the dinner one is giving, about the destiny of one's soul, about a railway journey or one's health, are all conflicts of opposing emotions. By such worries and restlessness of spirit we waste our strength and sap our vitality. By facing our conflicts and deliberately making our choice, by directing all our endeavours to one great purpose, confidently and fearlessly, the soul is restored again to harmony and strength.

THE CONVERSION OF THE INSTINCTS

Perhaps the most characteristic feature of a living being is, that is able to raise energy from a lower potential to a higher potential i.e. its efficiency for a given purpose is increased. In all *in*animate things energy, such as heat or motion, tends to be dissipated instead of being raised to a high potential. The human being can raise the energy contained in food and transform it into nerve energy, and by so doing he raises the potential of this form of energy. William James probably had in mind this difference of potential when he says: "Writing is higher than walking, thinking is higher than writing, deciding higher than thinking, deciding 'no' higher than deciding 'yes'." It is the intellectual and moral privilege of the human being that he can similarly raise the energy contained in the instincts, the radical fault in most of which is their selfish and egocentric character, to higher potentials; that is to say, by transforming the *quality* of this energy he raises its power to accomplish his ends, as sexual passion has been transformed into love; and by changing the *direction* of the energy he endows it with a greater effectiveness of *purpose*. By doing so he retains the power or force of the instincts, but directs that force to greater purpose. Furthermore, directed to altruistic ends, these individual instincts will no longer clash with the social instincts and thereby be deprived of strength, but co-operating and working in harmony with the social instincts they will be magnificently reinforced and their power multiplied

The *hunting instinct* affords an obvious illustration of this principle. We see its evolution in the transformation from the child's game of "hide and seek," to the keenness of the boy scout, until finally it assumes the form of exploration and discovery, its original object having been almost entirely forgotten.

Again, the instinct of *curiosity* is one of the potentialities of which are not sufficiently realised. We often use this term in a derogatory sense, as when one is said to be "inquisitive out of more curiosity." Curiosity often takes the form of prying into other people's affairs; it has driven more than one medical student I have known into morphinomania, and it leads many a young man and woman to sample those "thrills" which constitute "seeing life." "It is in their blood," we say, by which we imply that this impulse is instinctive. But this instinct of curiosity also gives the impulse to all true scientific pursuit. The instinct of curiosity directed towards human nature makes of one person a prying gossip, but leads another to search, like the psychologist, into the hidden depths of the human mind with sympathetic insight *i.e.* to increase its efficiency. Nothing short of a fundamental instinct could urge on the scientist to the researches which he pursues year after year, regardless of result or reward, to the great good of mankind.

The combative instinct – We often hear it maintained that the instinct of pugnacity which in the past has led to war must *necessarily* do so in the future, and that those who look for a permanent peace are therefore doomed to disappointment. This is a most unjustifiable assumption. Granting that the emotional element of every instinct must always remain, it is not necessary either that the same stimuli should awaken that emotion, or that the emotion could express itself in the same action – in this case, in slaughter. The instinct for combat finds expression in games such as football and in the rivalry of sport; and it is probably for this reason that the English people are less aggressive than other nations we know, though when the instinct is directed to war the Englishman throws himself into it with no less energy and zest. Long ago, William James pointed out the possibility of finding a moral equivalent of war in social service, from an egocentric to an altruistic and chivalrous end. We can take up arms for others even though we refuse to do so for ourselves. Then our instinct ceases to be aggressive, and becomes protective. So ultimately we shall learn that we can fight with other weapons for truth and purity, we shall join a crusade against oppression and vice – and this kind of combat will employ for social ends those emotions and instincts which at present we use for war and destruction. So we may confidently hope that the pugnacious instinct will find scope in fields of social service in the fight for justice, purity, and right.

[In the Great War men in this country were largely divided into those who fought because they hated the Hun and those who fought in chivalrous defence of the Belgian nation. The resultant action was the same, yet the motive for the impulse was very different, being the expression of a selfish instinct in one case and of an altruistic one in the other.]

It is often said that instincts are blind. It is rather we who are blind to their potency and to the purposes for which they exist. The abandonment of that false doctrine which would have us suppress them, and the substitution for it of an understanding of their proper uses, would open up to us resources of power which would give us in abundance energy and life.

Fear: Sex: Self-assertion – The instinctive emotion of fear and the instincts of sex and self-assertion deserve more detailed description on account of their great power – a power derived from their primitive character, their origin dating back to the earliest forms of animal life, but one far greater than the circumstances of modern life necessitate. Abolish these instincts and their effects in individual and social life, and the problems of mankind would be well-nigh solved. But abolish them we cannot; to suppress them is to deprive ourselves of their forces. To convert them and to redirect their forces to higher purposes is the work of beings possessed of intelligence, of will; and of an ideal.

The *instinctive emotion of fear*, so intimately associated with self-preservation, is one very necessary to our existence; without it we should soon be run down in the street. But the strength of this instinct is far greater than the uses of our civilised life require, for modern life is comparatively safe. There is a great deal of primitive fear that is left over, as it were, which we cannot use. The consequence is that the excess of fear tends to flow into wrong channels, or we fear excessively things which should rightly be objects of fear. Our surplus fear produces fear of poverty, fear of sickness and pain, fear of the future, fear of what might have been, fear of ourselves, fear of death, fear of life, fear of failure, and, perhaps most paralysing of all, fear of fear. If fear were abolished from modern life, the work of the psychotherapist would be nearly gone. It was not without cause that the Master of the soul so often reiterated "Fear not." "Be not afraid," "Be not anxious."

Is this, then, an instinct we should suppress? That is both impossible and desirable. The effects of fear are of two kinds: there is the fear that paralyses and the fear that inspires. Nothing paralyses our lives so much as fear, depriving them as it does of that abundance of power which is our birthright. But there is also the fear that nerves and inspires and expresses itself in the effective avoidance of imminent disaster. Now, we ask what constitutes the difference between the fear in these two cases? The answer is that fear paralyses when it offers now way of escape; it inspires when it is associated with hope. A hare, suddenly surprised, is either temporarily paralysed by fear, or stimulated to its topmost speed. It has been conjectured that the paralysis is probably a protective mechanism to enable the animal to hide when it cannot escape. If escape is possible the fear no longer paralyses, but is expressed in that tension of muscle, that alertness of mind, which make swift and effective action possible. Fear which includes a large element of hope passes into confidence, and this, as we have seen, is the first essential of power. If we apply our principle to what we have said concerning morbid fear, we can see that our problem is to turn the fear that paralyses into the fear that inspires. The fear of poverty inspires us to greater efforts, the fear of the future saves us from indolence, the fear of accident makes us alert; but this transformation takes place only when we have confidence that we can come through, and that the struggle will issue in victory.

Those who have raised discussion as to whether we should "fear God" have, I think, failed to appreciate this difference between the fear that paralyses and the fear akin to hope that urges us to active service. To fear God may mean that we are afraid of God because He may punish us, and in this case the fear is paralysing and brings forth no good result – "I knew thee, that thou wert an austere man. . . and hid thy talent in the ground." But the fear of God may mean that, in different to ourselves, we are filled with revert awe (in which emotion there is an element of fear), combined with a conviction of His willingness and power to help. This shifts the fear from ourselves, turns it into hope, and fills us with a confidence which stimulates us to great endeavours, and gives us that inspiration which only comes to those who humbly devote themselves to a noble cause.

The *sexual instinct* at first sight appears to be incapable of being raised to higher uses. It is an instinct which is necessary to the race for the purpose of reproduction. But, like fear, it has a far greater "affect" or emotional tone than we need for this purpose, and therefore its lavish expression apparently needs to be suppressed. On the other hand, the suppression of this instinct causes a very large number of the nervous ills to which men, and still more women, fall victims. But the sexual instinct, which naturally expresses itself as admiration for personal beauty, is probably at the basis of all the higher forms of art and may well be sublimated to this end. Further, this instinct is very closely associated with the maternal and paternal instincts, and seems almost to form an harmonious complex with them. The true lover is not only moved by the sexual instinct, but almost always associates with it the maternal or paternal instinct, and desires to "have someone to care for." [The intimate connection between the sexual instinct and the maternal instinct is demonstrated by the physiological co-operation between the physical organs corresponding respectively to these instincts.] Many a woman has married an invalid an simply in order to gratify this maternal instinct in caring for him. Unmarried women, in whom the sexual instincts are strong (and let them never be ashamed that these instincts *are* strong), may transform them into the maternal instinct in caring for children, "mothering" the lonely, or nursing the sick. The sexual instincts, debased to the uses of fleshly lust, kill the soul and stifle all noble thought and feeling; but from the same soil there may spring the stainless flower of love, whence comes all that is pure and holy in human life.

The *instinct of self-assertion*, when directed to purely individual ends, produces that aggressive character which is as offensive as it is anti-social. Nevertheless the opposite emotion of submission, if over-emphasised, results in a lack of practical initiative and independence. The virtue which corresponds to these excesses is not to be found in the "mean" between them, as Aristotle would say, but is the right direction of them both to altruistic ends. There is room for a new ethic on these lines. A self-assertion which forgets itself in the pursuit of a noble end is the truest humility. Submission that is self-conscious may be egoism disguised. True humility consists not in thinking little of oneself, but in not thinking of oneself at all. Thus both self-assertion and submissiveness are harmonised, and so lend the force of two combined instinctive emotions to the accomplishment of a noble end.

But more than that, the instinct of self-assertion is at the basis of the *sense of confidence* which I shall proceed to show is so essential to a life of power. Besides the intellectual acceptance of the idea "this is possible," confidence consists in the emotional reaction arising out of the instinct of self-assertion, "what is possible *I* can do," whether the confidence is based on the belief in my own power or in some other power on which I can rely.

CONFIDENCE AND FAITH

Confidence, deriving its power from the instinct of self-assertion, turns weakness into strength and failure into success.

"Somehow, when I started, I knew I was going to succeed." This is a phrase we often hear on the lips of a man flushed with success. He hardly realises that it was his confidence in success, his belief that he would succeed, that gave him the power to surmount his difficulties and win his way to victory. All round us we see men failing simply because they lack the confidence that they will succeed, while men with far less ability and talent, but with greater daring, carry off the prizes that life has to offer. It is not that the others do not try, but that they do not expect to succeed.

In the section on the will I quoted cases of men paralysed in arms and legs whom the will was quite impotent to restore to health; yet there was noting organically wrong with such patients. Why, then, were they paralysed? Why did not their strenuous efforts enable them to walk? Because they believed they could not move their limbs. They could say "I will," but *they had not learnt to say "I can."* The man paralysed in both legs would cling to me with such vigour that he nearly pulled me down with him – simply because he had not the confidence to trust himself to walk. In the hypnotic experiment on fatigue the subject could only grip 29 lbs. because he said "I am weak, I cannot grip it any harder." When he said, and believed, "I am strong and powerful," his strength was multiplied fivefold. I suddenly told another man that he could not talk; he tried, but found that he was dumb – simply because, being suggestible to my words, he lost confidence in his power to speak, and believed what I suggested to be in fact true. In all such cases we have seen that the will alone does not ensure success. "To will is present with me, but how to perform I know not." That which is lacking is "confidence."

I have spoken of the paralysing effects of fear. Confidence removes this paralysis and turns belief into a mighty impulse to act. It fills men with the strength which makes the soul master of its fate. It possesses the timid who cling to the shores of life, who have toiled all night and caught nothing, and bids them launch out into the deep, where endeavour is crowned with overwhelming success. Want of belief in its possibility is always the main obstacle to the performing of any mighty work. Faith in its possibility – a faith not necessarily founded on evidence but one that dares to take the risk – is the greatest asset to success in any task. "If thou canst?" "All things are possible to them that believe."

THE EXPENDITURE OF POWER

Nature is economic in her gifts; she will not give strength to those who will not expend it. These remain uninspiring and uninspired. She is lavish in her gifts to those who will use them, and especially to those who devote them to nature's altruistic ends, for such ends harmonise the soul. Life demands expression. If the life-stream that flows through us finds the channel blocked by a life of inactivity, we inevitably suffer from staleness and boredom, or a sense of physical debility. A purposeless life is a life of fatigue. We all know from personal experience how tired we may become while doing nothing, but let us once find an outlet for our energies, some object upon which to expend them, and our instinctive powers awake us to life. Mental fatigue, as we have already said, is due not to exhaustion but to stagnation. The Sea of Galilee is fresh and blue, it gives life to living creatures within its sunlit waters – not because it receives waters, but because it gives of them freely. The Dead Sea is dead, not because there is not supply of fresh water, but because it permits no outlet. It is therefore stagnant and deadly; no fish lives in its waters, nor is any beast to be found upon its shores. It is a law of nature – a law of life – that only by giving shall we receive. None is so healthy and fresh as he who gives freely of his strength, and thereby liberates his impulses and instinctive powers into quickened activity. This is of immense practical importance. In the treatment of neurasthenia, the chief symptom of which is fatigue it is often found that the "Weird Mitchell" treatment of inactivity and isolation is the worst a physican can prescribe. Already is the patient suffering from too much self-consciousness and introspection. Some disappointment or sorrow may have taken all the life out of him: the zeal and keenness of his life has suddenly gone. In popular language, what he needs is "something to take him out of himself"; something to interest him, some object which will liberate the forces pent up in his soul. Give such a man "something to live for," that awakens his interest, and his ambition will arouse his instinctive emotions till the heart that was sluggish palpitates with the joy of life once more, the nerves tingle with eager expectation. Life's demand for expression will be satisfied.

How wonderful is the way in which, with quite ordinary folk, power leaps to our aid in any time of emergency. We lead timid lives, shrinking from difficult tasks till perhaps we are forced into them or ourselves determine on them, and immediately we seem to unlock the unseen forces. When we have to face danger, then courage comes; when trial puts a long-continued strain upon us, we find ourselves possessed by the power to endure; or when disaster ultimately brings the fall which we so long dreaded, we feel underneath us the strength as of the everlasting arms. Common experience teaches that, when great demands are made upon us, if only we fearlessly accept the challenge and confidently expend our strength, every danger or difficulty brings its own strength – "As thy days so shall thy strength be."

ENERGY AND REST

In considering the causes of fatigue we found that the mental factor played a very prominent part. The main causes of such fatigue were over-sensitiveness to ordinary physical fatigue, the conviction of weakness, and the conflict of will and emotions or of the emotions with themselves. A life of purposeful and altruistic activity will rid us of that habit of introspection which produces the first form of fatigue: the sense of confidence will drive away thoughts of weakness; and we have now to deal with the third form, conflict within the mind, the most characteristic form of which is worry and anxiety. This is to be met, firstly, by discovering and bringing into consciousness the latent cause of our worry, which normally tends to elude consciousness. Modern practice in psychotherapy confirms the old belief that confession, more especially confession of fears and anxieties, is good for the soul. The "letting out" of the "repressed complex" is itself often sufficient to cure; secondly, by converting the instincts and directing their energies toward useful and harmonious ends; and, thirdly, by cultivating a *restfulness of mind* which is the counterpart of a life of energy.

Weakness results from the wastage caused by restlessness of mind. Power comes from a condition of mental quietude. The secret of energy is to learn to keep the mind at rest, even in the multitude of life's activities. Look at this patient suffering from neurasthenia. He complains that he is suffering from fatigue; but there is another symptom you notice about him – he is irritable, cannot stand noises, cannot bear to be crossed or disturbed. The fatigue and the irritability are part of the same trouble. It is a characteristic of nervous patients that they are always restless: they tell you that they must always be doing something, always be "on the go." They cannot concentrate, they cannot remember. They are in a state of perpetual motion. They are worried and anxious, fret and are irritable, until, through sheer exhaustion of mind, they drift into the most characteristic condition of the neurasthenic, that of fatigue. And if it is not surprising that such men become fatigued. The average neurasthenic is ordered to take a rest in the afternoon, but he spends the time in reading the paper; he goes to bed early at night, but sits up reading a novel. He gives his body more rest than it needs, failing to realise that what the body needs is not relaxation but re-invigoration. At the same time he never permits his mind that rest which alone can enable in to invigorate the body. It is characteristic of the neurasthenic that in the morning, possibly after a long night's sleep, he wakes up more fatigued than he went to bed; for though his body has had many hours' rest, his mind has been restless and perturbed even in sleep.

This art of resting the mind and the power of dismissing from it all care and worry is probably one of the secrets of energy in our great men. It is generally said that Edison, the inventor, finds four hours' sleep sufficient for his needs and that he works for eighteen hours. If that is the case, I can conceive him as a man whose mind, in spite of the nature of his work, has the power of banishing all the problems and difficulties of the day. This, I understand, was also one of the secrets of the energy of Gladstone, and probably also of many other great men who have the power to free their minds entirely from the business of the day in dreamless sleep. Look into the face of Napoleon and, besides the cruelty there, you will see that perfect composure and calm which stamps him as a man of great reserve power.

[It is interesting to note that, even physiologically, Napoleon was constructed with a power of rest shared by few men, for he had a pulse rate of only about 50 compared with the normal rate of 75.]

The mental and moral strain that some men have to undergo seems incredible. In the course of a day the President, for instance, guides the counsels of state, directs wars, settles industrial disputes, and conducts diplomatic relations with other nations, all in addition to the ordinary cares of his private affairs. Compare his output of energy with that, say, of his barber, whose anxieties are confined to his little shop, whose disputes are concerned only with his two assistants, and whose diplomacy reaches its height in his attempt to persuade you to buy his hair lotion without suggesting that you are bald. Yet, if you observe these two men at the close of day, probably the President is the less fatigued of the two. The thing that strikes us is that, however much energy such a man expends, there always seems to be an ample resupply which keeps him vigorous and fresh.

At the present time I am treating each morning about twenty neurasthenic patients at once by hypnotic suggestion. I always commence treatment by suggestions of quietness and calmness of mind, of freedom from anxiety and the passing away of all nervousness and fear. To attempt to stimulate a restless and worried mind with energetic suggestions is as futile as whipping a dying horse. When the mind is quiet and rested, only then do I suggest thoughts of vigour of mind, strength of body, and determination of will. Inspiring, stimulating thoughts, falling on a mind calm and receptive, draw from its silent depths ample resources of strength which produce calmness and peace. The confidence and happiness with which these men rise from their half-hour's rest is a proof that this rest, unlike the neurasthenic's ordinary night's "rest," has brought them into touch with untold resources of power.

The art of alternating rest and activity is an art well worth acquiring. Some people have the power of putting themselves to sleep for five or ten minutes at any time of the day. This carries with it the power of dismissing from the mind at any time all cares, which forthwith

> fold up their tents like the Arabs and silently steal away.

Night time should be reserved for sleep, and no thoughts of the day should be permitted to break into the preserves of sleep.

I once put into a short hypnotic sleep a patient, tremulous, anxious, sleepless. When he awakened he spontaneously remarked that that was the best sleep he had for months, and on being questioned replied that he thought he had slept for several hours, whereas, in point of fact, he had slept only a few minutes. During those few moments he had had a perfect control over a mind worried with anxious thoughts.

That the life of energy is dependent on the art of resting is one of the fundamental laws of physiology as well as of psychology. The alteration of rest and work is necessary for the activity of life. Even the heart is not always active, as is sometimes supposed; it has its periods of repose at the end of each beat when there is a relaxation, which is sufficient though it lasts only the fraction of a second, to refresh it for the next beat. In the last section we mentioned the fact that a nerve was practically unfatiguable. That fact is not due to there being no wastage, for the nerve tissue is always being used up; as Waller says, the nerve "is inexhaustible, not because there is little or no expenditure, but because there is an ample re-supply." The nerve rests for only a very small fraction of a second between the electric shocks which pass along it, yet in that moment of rest it is able to draw upon that ample re-supply which reinvigorates it to renewed activity. These physiological principles point the way to find refreshment of the mind. There are ample resources of power at our disposal, but in the course of our life we need moments of mental rest when the soul can go apart and rest awhile. Life, like music, has its rhythm of silence as well as of sound; it has its crests of surging energy, and its quiet calm in the trough of the wave. Life has its moments of throbbing energy, but needs also its moments of relaxation. The restful life does not demand that we withdraw from the world in ascetic retreat; but it demands such a control of our thoughts and feelings that, even when active in body, we can have that quiescence of mind which is itself the most perfect rest.

> And out of that tranquility shall rise
> The end and healing of our earthly pains,
> Since the mind governed is the mind at rest

THE SOURCE OF ENERGY

This Essay has raised the question as to whether our strength comes from within ourselves, in which case we may be conceived as a reservoir of energy, or whether it is derived from an outside source, using us as a channel for its activity. (1) It is true that we do store up a certain amount of energy derived, physiologically, from the nutriment of food and air, physiologically, from the myriads of impressions of sight, sound, and touch, which are continually falling upon our senses and being recorded and stored, probably in the lower brain centres. (2) But what we have been especially considering are not these acquired energies, but the great hereditary instinctive powers which have borne down like a wave through humanity from generation to generation. (3) Several of the greatest psychologists, and, in particular those clinical psychologists who have to deal with the actual diseases of men, have tended towards the view that the source of power is to be regarded as some impulse that works through us, and is not of our own making. What Janet calls "mental energy" is a force which ebbs in the neurasthenic and flows in the healthy man: Jung speaks of *libido* or *urge* as a force which surges through our lives, now as an impulse towards nutrition, now as the sexual instinct; there is also the *èlan vital* of Bergson. These views suggest that we are not merely receptacles but *channels* of energy. Life and power is not so much contained in us, it *courses through* us. Man's might is not to be measured by the stagnant water in the well, but by the limitless supply from the clouds of heaven. These descriptive theories represent man as borne on the crest of an impulse which he can only partially control. Whether we are to look upon this impulse as cosmic energy, as a lifeforce, or what may be its relation to the Divine immanence in Nature, it is for other investigators to say. It is the business of the philosopher to speculate upon the ultimate nature of reality. The scientist has merely to study the laws of its manifestation in concrete expression. I merely wish to point out that the views expressed above as to the derivation of our human energies from the instinctive emotions does not exclude the foregoing or any other theories as to their *ultimate* sources, which is yet a matter of speculation.

THE DYNAMIC OF RELIGION

While it has not been the purpose of this Essay to deal with questions of theology, I cannot help pointing out that our discussion of the psychology of power has a very direct bearing on the question of *the dynamic of religion*, and especially on the power possessed by the Christian religion of liberating energies which can transform the living soul into a quickening spirit. In its fundamental doctrine of love to God and man, Christianity harmonises the emotions of the soul into one inspiring purpose, thereby abolishing all conflict, and liberating instead of suppressing the free energies of men. In its doctrine of the Spirit it emphasises the element of power in religion. No reader of the New Testament can fail to be struck by the constant reiteration in different forms of the idea that the normal experience of a Christian at that epoch was enhancement of power – "I can do all things" – an enhancement attributed by them to the operation in and through them of a Divine energy to which the community gave the name of the "Spirit" – "Ye shall receive power." Pentecost, the healing miracles of the Apostolic Age, the triumphant progress of the religion through the Roman Empire, the heroic deeds of saints and martyrs, – all these point to the sense of a power newly discovered. In contrast, looking at the Church of to-day, one cannot but be struck with its powerlessness. It contains men of intellect; it produces a type of piety and devotion which one cannot but admire; it sacrifices itself in works of kindness and beneficence; but even its best friends would not claim what it inspires in the world the sense of power. What strikes one rather is its impotence and failure. This want of inspiration and power is associated with the fact that men no longer believe in the existence of the Spirit in any effective practical way. They believe in God the Father, and they are reverent; they believe in the Son, and the Church numbers amongst its members millions who humbly try to "follow in His steps"; but for all practical purposes they are like that little band at Ephesus who had "not so much as heard whether there be any Holy Ghost," and, lacking the inspiration of such a belief, they were weak and wonder why.

In this place I need only indicate the close connection between restfulness of mind, so essential to the cure of nervous ills, and that characteristic of religious devotion. "They that *wait* on the Lord shall *renew* their strength." There is the alternation of repose and work, and the insistence on the source of strength being a psychical and not a physical character. Christianity also teaches that to learn to rest, not only in moments snatched from our work but by keeping a mind free from worry and anxiety, neither caring for the morrow nor fearful of the forgiven past, is to give ourselves the opportunity of drawing on that "ample re-supply" which comes to those who do not fear to expend their energy for others. Life will throb within and through us, but our souls will be in repose.

The religious writings of men of old constantly emphasised confidence and cheerfulness as the keynote to strength. "In quietness and confidence shall be your strength." "Let not your heart be troubled." "Be not anxious." "Be of good cheer, I have overcome the world." "Say unto them of a fearful heart, 'Be strong, fear not'." Such words as the following are literally fulfilled before our eyes in a shell-shock hospital of the present day. "The eyes of the blind shall be opened, and the ears of the deaf be unstopped. Then shall the lame man leap as an hart and the tongue of the dumb shall sing. They shall obtain gladness and joy, and sorrow and sighing shall flee away." Accurately and wonderfully these words describe both the treatment by the suggestion of confidence and its effects, as well on the body as on the mind.

This power which the Church has lost is being rediscovered, but along different lines. The psychotherapist, who is a physician of the soul, has been compelled to acknowledge the validity of the practical principles of the Christian religion, though he may or may not accept the doctrines on which they are said to be based.

Speaking as a student of psychotherapy, who, a such, has no concern with theology, I am convinced that the Christian religion is one of the most valuable and potent influences that we possess for producing that harmony and peace of mind and that confidence of soul which is needed to bring health and power to a large proportion of nervous patients. In some cases I have attempted to cure nervous patients with suggestions of quietness and confidence, but without success until I have linked these suggestions on to that faith in the power of God which is the substance of the Christian's confidence and hope. Then the patient has become strong.

[Lest this should be considered a prejudiced view I quote from Jung (Analytical Psychology): "I have come to the conclusion that these religious and philosophical motive forces – the so-called metaphysical needs of the human being – must receive positive consideration at the hands of the analyst (physician)... he must make them serve biological ends as psychologically valuable factors. Thus these instincts assume once more those functions that have been theirs from time immemorial." Again in a volume entitled *The Christian Religion as a Healing Power* (E. Worcester and others), I find quoted some weighty opinions. Möbius, the neurologist, says: "The consciousness of being within the hand of Providence, the confident hope of future righteousness and redemption, is a support to the believer in his work, his care and his need, for which unbelief has no compensation. If we consider the effect of irreligion as increasing our helplessness to resist the storms of life, its relation to nervousness cannot be doubted." "Religious faith," says Dubois of Berne, himself an agnostic, "would be the best preventative against the maladies of the soul and the most powerful means of curing them, if it had sufficient life to create true Christian stoicism in its followers. Feeling himself upheld by his God, he fears neither sickness nor death... he remains unshaken in the midst of his sufferings, and is inaccessible to the cowardly emotions of nervous people." Dr. Clouston of Edinburgh, the specialist in mental diseases, says, "to treat of the hygiene of the mind, without including a consideration of the religious instinct and its effects, would be to omit one of its most powerful factors."]

I have tried to show that the experience of applied psychology, especially psychotherapy, points toward the conclusion that we are living far below the limits of our possible selves, and that there are open to us resources of power, available through the right use of our instincts, which, if directed to noble purposes, will free our minds from those worries, anxieties, and morbid fatigue which spoil our lives, and will free us for a life of energy and strength.

In the course of my argument I have indicated directions which this line of investigation cannot but affect the theory and practice of religion: to have done more than indicate directions might have seemed presumptuous in one who speaks as a student of science rather than a philosopher or theologian. I hope however, that I have made it clear that few things would be of more value, whether for medical science, for everyday conduct, or for religion, than such a re-interpretation of some of the fundamental beliefs of Christianity as would make them intellectually possible of acceptance to the modern man. And Psychology has opened up lines along which one may look to see effected that reconciliation between science and religion, the attempt to procure which led to an impasse a generation ago because "science" was taken almost exclusively to mean physical science. But whilst psychology has helped us to solve many problems, it has raised others – for instance, the relation of suggestion to prayer or the view that all religion, including our idea of God, is subjective. So true is this that it appears as though the next great conflict in religion will be in the realm of psychology, as in the last generation it was in the realm of biology and the theory of evolution. To my mind the issue will be the same, that moral and religious thought will need to be greatly modified, but that it will at the same time be greatly enriched. The main object, however, of the Essay has been practical – to show that there are resources of power at the disposal of all. But the fact that so many seek for power and yet do not receive it suggests that piety is not the only requisite of power. To obtain it we must obey the higher laws of nature, and in particular make use of the forces we already find at our human disposal; and fearlessly expanding them in a spirit of confidence for the fulfillment of our ideals, we shall harmonise mind, will, and emotion in one throbbing impulse of life and power.

Taking, then, the instincts in their cruder form as handed down to us by our brutish ancestry, we should seek not to suppress them, but to use the powers which lie latent in them. We may transform where we cannot suppress, and, by aid of reason and the higher emotions, re-direct the lower instincts to noble purposes. We need not obstruct, but press into our service, the passions of the soul; we can fill our sails with the very winds and gales which threaten the shipwreck of our lives; tap the resources of the lightning which ruthlessly destroys, and turn its electric power into the driving-force of our enterprises.

Printed in Poland
by Amazon Fulfillment
Poland Sp. z o.o., Wrocław